Leaders on Leading

Leaders on
Leading

Insights from the Field

Foreword by Larry E. Senn

LEADERSHIP PRESS

LOS ANGELES, NEW YORK, LONDON

A **Leadership Press** book,
published by arrangement with the authors.

Library of Congress Catalog Card Number: 99-091340

ISBN 0-9648466-6-7 (softcover)
First printing, October 1999

Printed in Canada

printing number
1 2 3 4 5 6 7 8 9 0

Acknowledgements

We would like to thank all those who helped with the compilation and
production of this book. They included Larry Senn, John Childress, Jim
Hart, Chris Choppin, Peter Brown, Sam Schultz, John Cole, Bonnie Norris,
and Janet Rasmussen. Their contributions are greatly appreciated.

Distributed by:

Gulf Publishing Company

4900 Campbell Road, Houston, TX 77041   (713) 520-4444

Table of Contents

Foreword by Larry E. Senn   vii

1   Mindful Leadership   1

2   Taking Action   21

3   Tapping Business Wisdom   37

4   Making the Decision   47

5   Accountability and
     Responsibility   57

6   Principles and Values   65

7   The Shadow of the Leader   89

8   Goals and Resolution   99

9   The Current of Change   119

10   Interactions, Teamwork,
         and Strategies   129

11   Living in a Complex World   145

12   Reflections and Beliefs   159

13   The Enterprising   173

Author Index   181

About Senn-Delaney Leadership
         Consulting Group   196

Foreword

by Larry E. Senn

INSPIRATION AND INSIGHT play a role in the lives of all great leaders. Both can be found in various ways including nature and by examining the deeper thoughts of others. Therefore, a book of quotations should be like a still spring-fed lake surrounded by towering pines, or crashing ocean waves on a sandy tropical beach. There should be something there to inspire everyone. *Leaders on Leading* is a collection of quotes we have gathered over the years for our seminars and our work in coaching leaders. They have found their way onto the pages of our publications, and have been located specifically for this little book. They are intended to provide insight and inspiration for a generation of leaders who, because of today's hectic business pace, must often look for a concise vision that helps them describe the world they encounter. They are also offered as a means to furnish practical advice from past leaders to those at work in the present.

The quotes that follow are often eloquent, profound, and sometimes funny expressions of what we historically know about leadership. They are offered here not as an exhaustive attempt to capture everything ever uttered about leadership, but as reminders of what leadership promises, demands, and ultimately delivers.

Those of us in positions of leadership frequently find ourselves in lonely places, which might be uncharted within our realms of experience. That doesn't mean someone else hasn't been there before us. Sometimes, finding a level of comfort in the unknown requires nothing more than recognizing that others have preceded our efforts and have left a signpost along the way. Other times, by finding a place of humility, where we acknowledge we don't have all the answers, new and unexpected possibilities can emerge.

Leaders on Leading was composed to satisfy these and many other issues leaders continually face. The book has been divided into topics that all of us encounter and in which others have also tread. Like our still forest lake, they can provide a way to both reflect and renew our commitment to the job of leading others. These quotes can also provide just enough space away from a pressing problem to allow the necessary and novel solution to surface. Wisdom is rarely time dependent. It arises when we are able to reflect and quiet our minds. It is our intent that this collection offer the opportunity for reflection as well as entertainment. I have often been amazed by what speaks to me when I pick up a quote book, let go of a little control, open it at random, and select a quote on a page.

I hope you find these "insights from the field" as useful and illuminating as I do. Enjoy them for what they are—a healthy helping of our collective wisdom on leadership.

—Larry E. Senn

Mindful Leadership

Mindful Leadership addresses the thinking of the leader and how that level of thinking shapes his or her behaviors in either a healthy or dysfunctional manner. These quotes speak to the heart and mind of the leader, and the level of awareness that is required to conduct business in today's constantly evolving and reshaping marketplace.

Society is the relationship between you and me; and if our relationship is based on ambition, each one of us wanting to be more powerful than the other, then obviously we shall always be in conflict.

—J. Krishnamurti

The wise leader is of service: receptive, yielding, following. The group member's vibration dominates and leads, while the leader follows. But soon it is the member's consciousness which is transformed. It is the job of the leader to be aware of the group member's process; it is the need of the group member to be received and paid attention to. Both get what they need, if the leader has the wisdom to serve and follow.

—John Heider

Not knowing, that is, being willing to admit that we don't know, is one of the keys that opens the door to creative intelligence. It takes humility to open that door. Our ego doesn't like not knowing and would prefer to go over and over what we already think and believe rather than trust in a subtle, unknown process like creative intelligence.

—Richard Carlson and Joseph Bailey

It is interesting that the words "whole" and "health" come from the same root (the Old English *hal,* as in "hale and hearty"). So it should come as no surprise that the unhealthiness of our world today is in direct proportion to our inability to see it as a whole.

—Peter M. Senge

...the courage to adhere to the truth as we learn it involves, then, the courage to face ourselves, with the clear admission of all the mistakes we have made—mistakes are sins only when not admitted.

—Buckminster Fuller

Listening well, the key to empathy, is also crucial to competence in communicating. Listening skills—asking astute questions, being open-minded and understanding, not interrupting, seeking suggestions—account for about a third of people's evaluations of whether someone they work with is an effective communicator.

—Daniel Goleman

Humility is the Queen without whom none can checkmate the divine King.

—Saint Teresa of Avila

Humility + Wonder = Wisdom.

—Author unknown

The best way to establish rapport with someone is to assume that you don't have it.

—Richard Carlson

...an intelligent mind is one which is constantly learning, never concluding.

—J. Krishnamurti

All feelings derive and become alive, whether negative or positive, from the power of *Thought*.

Thought is not reality; yet it is through Thought that our realities are created. It is what we as humans put into our *thoughts,* that dictates what we think of life.

—Sydney Banks

The way of cowardice is to embed ourselves in a cocoon, in which we perpetuate our habitual patterns. When we are constantly recreating our basic patterns of behavior and thought, we never have to leap into fresh air or onto fresh ground.

—Chögyam Trungpa

We all have the capacity to call a time-out and recognize our thinking—to see that thought is not an absolute reality but merely our experience of reality in the moment. This process of self-awareness, or thought recognition, is perhaps the most powerful tool we have to restore our mental health.

—Richard Carlson and Joseph Bailey

Things themselves don't hurt or hinder us. Nor do other people. How we view these things is another matter. It is our attitudes and reactions that give us trouble.... We cannot choose our external circumstances, but we chose how we respond to them.

—Epictetus

Team learning develops the skills of groups of people to look for the larger picture that lies beyond individual perspectives. The personal mastery fosters the personal motivation to continually learn how our actions affect our world.

—Peter M. Senge

Great inventors and discoverers seem to have made their discoveries and inventions as it were by the way, in the course of their everyday life.

—Elizabeth Rundle Charles

Once the closed system of rules enters consciousness, thought begins to serve the rules. The brain-mind seems to give up its creative and formative functions and shifts to maintenance.

—Bob Samples

The negative effects of thought arise when we lose sight of thought recognition—when we forget that we are thinking and that our thinking is creating our experience.

—Richard Carlson and Joseph Bailey

There is nothing either good or bad but thinking makes it so.

—William Shakespeare

The moment you criticize, you are not in relationship, you already have a barrier between yourself and them; but if you merely observe, then you will have a direct relationship with people and with things.

—J. Krishnamurti

The primary rule of interpretation is that all meaning is context-bound.

—Ken Wilber

I've worked while my mind is spinning every which way and while my mind is very focused —and I can tell you with absolute certainty that a focused mind is more relaxed, creative, and efficient than one that is scattered.

—Richard Carlson

We are not separate from Being, we are in it...

—Plotinus

The best way to make your dreams come true
is to wake up.

—Paul Valery

Our own life is the instrument with which we
experiment with the truth.

—Thich Nhat Hanh

Just sheer life cannot be said to have a purpose, because look at all the different purposes it has all over the place. But each incarnation, you might say, has a potentiality, and the mission of life is to live that potentiality. How do you do it? My answer is, "Follow your bliss." There's something inside you that knows when you're in the center, that knows when you're on the beam or off the beam.

—Joseph Campbell and Bill Moyers

There is a wonderful mystical law of nature that the three things we crave most in life —happiness, freedom, and peace of mind— are attained by giving them to someone else.

—Lawrence Stern

We need to find the link between our traditions and our present experience of life. Nowness, or the magic of the present moment, is what joins the wisdom of the past with the present.

—Chögyam Trungpa

If an experience is contaminated by the past it is merely a continuity of the past, and therefore not an original experience.

—J. Krishnamurti

I learned early that one of the most important qualities of a leader is listening without judgment, or with what Buddhists call *bare attention.*

—Phil Jackson

To create a bridge between your spirituality and your work means that you take the essence of who you are and what you believe into your daily work life.... It means that if kindness, patience, honesty, and generosity are spiritual qualities that you believe in, you make every effort to practice those qualities at work.

—Richard Carlson

The supreme accomplishment is to blur the line between work and play.

—Arnold Toynbee

Empathy is crucial for wielding influence; it is difficult to have a positive impact on others without first sensing how they feel and understanding their position. People who are poor at reading emotional cues and inept at social interactions are very poor at influence. The first step in influence is building rapport.

—Daniel Goleman

Nothing can bring you peace but yourself.

—Ralph Waldo Emerson

Every man stamps his value on himself ...man is made great or small by his own will.

—J. C. F. von Schiller

He who seeks for applause only from without
has all his happiness in another's keeping.

—Oliver Goldsmith

Not in the shouts and plaudits of the throng,
but in ourselves, are triumph and defeat.

—Henry Wadsworth Longfellow

We carry with us the wonders we seek
without us.

—Thomas Browne

Ruin and recovery are both from within.

—Epictetus

Man is not the creature of circumstances.
Circumstances are the creatures of men.

—Benjamin Disraeli

The only Zen you find on the tops of mountains
is the Zen you bring up there.

—Robert M. Pirsig

Strategy is important. But once you've done
the mental work, there comes a point when
you have to throw yourself into the action and
put your heart on the line. That means not
only being brave, but also being compassion-
ate, toward yourself, your teammates, and
your opponents.

—Phil Jackson

Being caught up in a strong consuming mood
is a roadblock to smooth interaction. If we
enter into a conversation while preoccupied
by a strong mood, the other person is likely to
experience us as being unavailable, or what
the sociologist Irving Goffman has called
"away"—just going through the motions of
the conversation while obviously distracted.

—Daniel Goleman

The basic misunderstanding about the notion
of empowerment is that it can be bestowed on
someone, like a Knighthood. No! *The only person who can empower me is me.* Others can
provide a conducive environment or atmos-
phere where I can function in an "empow-
ered" or more responsible way.

—Dan Miller

We always have a choice: we can limit our perception so that we close off vastness, or we can allow vastness to touch us. When we draw down the power and depth of vastness into a single perception, then we are discovering and invoking magic. By magic we do not mean unnatural power over the phenomenal world, but rather the discovery of innate or primordial wisdom in the world as it is.

—Chögyam Trungpa

You need to start trusting yourself enough to know that when you need an answer or an idea, quieting your mind—instead of filling it with data—may provide the best possible answer or solution.

—Richard Carlson

...where there is fear there is no intelligence.... To live is to find out for yourself what is true, and you can do this only when there is freedom, when there is continuous revolution inwardly, within yourself.

—J. Krishnamurti

Initiating and taking action is the responsibility of the leader. The quotes that follow address such areas as how active leadership creates direction, the manner in which it inspires others to act, and the courage needed to move forward.

We need men who can dream of things that never were.

—John F. Kennedy

No one knows what he can do till he tries.

—Publilius Syrus

Man cannot accept certainties; he must discover them.

—John Middleton Murry

Worthwhile advances are seldom made without taking risks.

—W. I. Beveridge

We are in one of those great historical periods that occur every 200 to 300 years when people don't understand the world anymore, and the past is not sufficient to explain the future. We are in a period of time in which companies will have to innovate quickly and be global to succeed.

—Peter F. Drucker

The mind, like a parachute, functions only when open.

—Author unknown

It is only during the storm that we truly become sailors.

—John R. Childress

Nothing ever succeeds which exuberant spirits have not helped produce.

—Friedrich Wilhelm Nietzsche

You can begin the process of eliminating negative emotions by simply refusing to justify them.

—Brian Tracy

Real generosity to the future lies in giving all to the present.

—Albert Camus

If you do not know where you are going, every road will get you nowhere.

—Henry Kissinger

What each man does is based not on direct and certain knowledge, but on pictures made by himself or given to him.... The way in which the world is imagined determines at any particular moment what men will do.

—Walter Lippmann

Dreams have as much influence as actions.

—Stéphane Mallarmé

If you can dream it, you can do it.

—Walt Disney

The more you allow yourself to be dreamy-
eyed and to fantasize, the more you will be
able to change your life for the better.

—Wayne Dyer

In the long run men hit only what they aim at.

—Henry David Thoreau

Don't wait for your ship to come in; swim
out to it.

—Author unknown

The businesses that succeed are those that are first within an industry to see an adjacent possibility and act upon it.

—Howard Sherman and Ron Schultz

There is one thing stronger than all the armies of the world, and that is an idea whose time has come.

—Victor Hugo

The real challenge is to maintain the course of change, and the key difference between winners and losers is their resolve to do so.

—Daryl R. Conner

A person always doing his or her best becomes a natural leader, just by example.

—Joe DiMaggio

The man who complains about the way the ball bounces is likely the one who dropped it.

—Lou Holtz

Seize the day; put no trust in the morrow!

—Horace

I shut my eyes in order to see.

—Paul Gauguin

Force without mind falls by its own weight.

—Horace

Life is what happens when you've planned something else.

—M. Scott Peck

The leaders of today's hottest companies don't stop to deliberate. They act—and at top speed.

—Geoffrey Colvin

While we stop to think, we often miss our opportunity.

—Publilius Syrus

You see things; and you say, "Why?" But I dream things that never were; and I say, "Why not?"

—George Bernard Shaw

Not the cry, but the flight of the wild duck, leads the flock to fly and follow.

—Chinese proverb

...one thing that distinguishes high performers, is that they take responsibility for their own lives. If things aren't going well, they do something about it. They don't feel themselves victimized or powerless.

—Jerry Fletcher

Eighty percent of success is showing up.

—Woody Allen

Chiefly the mold of a man's fortune is in his own hands.

—Francis Bacon

We must adjust to changing times and still hold to unchanging principles.

—Jimmy Carter

Those who make the worst use of their time are the first to complain of its brevity.

—Jean de la Bruyère

I definitely am going to take a course in time
management …just as soon as I can work it
into my schedule.

—Louis E. Boone

Dost thou love life? Then do not squander time;
for that's the stuff life is made of.

—Benjamin Franklin

Successful people are willing to do things
other people won't.

—Sally Behn

It looks impossible until you do it, and then you find it possible.

—Evelyn Underhill

If customers think you have a high level of expertise and it can help them, you're worth more to them.

—Mark Landiak

Cherish forever what makes you unique, 'cuz you're really a yawn if it goes!

—Bette Midler

It had long since come to my attention that people of accomplishment rarely sat back and let things happen to them. They went out and happened to things.

—Elinor Smith

A success is one who decided to succeed …and worked. A failure is one who decided to succeed …and wished.

—William Arthur Ward

The extra mile will have no traffic jams.

—Author unknown

Many people wait for something to happen or someone to take care of them. But people who end up with good jobs are the proactive ones who are solutions to problems, not problems themselves, who seize the initiative to do whatever is necessary, consistent with correct principles, to get the job done.

—Stephen R. Covey

What does not kill me makes me stronger.

—Albert Camus

Heroism consists of hanging on one minute longer.

—Norwegian proverb

Time is the measure of business.

—Francis Bacon

God give them wisdom that have it; and those
that are fools, let them use their
talents.

—William Shakespeare

In empathic listening, you listen with your eyes
and with your heart, you use your right brain
as well as your left. You sense, you intuit, you
feel. Empathic listening is powerful because it
gives you accurate data to work with.

—Stephen R. Covey

3 Tapping Business Wisdom

What wisdom can leaders share about their common experience? How does a leader tap into his or her own wisdom while accessing the wisdom that can be gathered from the field. Leaders speak to us again and again that leading a large corporation is virtually impossible for one person. Here is some of the collective wisdom we have gathered from our field and others.

In the beginner's mind there are many possibilities, but in the expert's there are few.

—Shunryu Suzuki

The answer to today's business and personal challenges does not lie in harder or more frantic effort. We believe it lies in creating an organization in which things happen with greater ease, one with more collaboration instead of turf, and wiser, more thoughtful, decisions.

—Larry E. Senn and John R. Childress

A company is known by the people it keeps.

—Author unknown

Too many businessmen never stop to ponder what they are doing, they reject the need for self-discipline; they are satisfied to be clever, when they need to be wise.

—Louis Finkelstein

People, products, profits ...if we take care of our people, products will be created, and profits will follow.

—Jerry Sanders

In the end, all business operations can be reduced to three words: people, product, and profits.

—Lee Iacocca

Innovation comes in two forms: the shocking new solution, and the one in front of your nose.

—Kevin Strehlo

Employees are not interchangeable resources that can replace one another at will.

—Kathy Kolbe

Golden Rule principles are just as necessary for operating a business profitably as are trucks, typewriters, or twine.

—James Cash Penney

Problems are only opportunities in work
clothes.

—Henry J. Kaiser

I remember that a wise friend of mine did usually say, " That which is everybody's
 business is nobody's business."

—Izaak Walton

You can't create an emotional tie to a bad
product because it's not honest.

—Philip Knight

Many companies view each negotiation as a separate situation. But companies that take a more coordinated approach are making better deals and forging stronger relationships.

—Danny Ertol

Do not anticipate trouble, or worry about what may never happen. Keep in the sunlight.

—Benjamin Franklin

There is nothing so easy but that it becomes difficult when you do it reluctantly.

—Publius Terentius Afer

He that is good at making excuses is seldom good at anything else.

—Benjamin Franklin

That is what learning is. You suddenly understand something you've understood all your life, but in a new way.

—Doris Lessing

It's very hard to surgically prick a balloon. You may let out a lot more air than you bargained for.

—Alan Blinder

To err is human, but it is against company policy.

—Author unknown

Those who stand for nothing fall for anything.

—Alexander Hamilton

The method of enterprising is to plan with audacity, and execute with vigor; to sketch out a map of possibilities; and then to treat them as probabilities.

—Courtland Bovee

Business should be fun. Without fun, people are left wearing emotional raincoats most of their working lives. Building fun into business is vital; it brings life into our daily being ...we should not relegate it to something we buy after work with money we earn.

—Michael Phillips

Business will be better or worse.

—Author unknown

To do two things at once is to do neither.

—Publilius Syrus

The shortest way to do many things is to do
only one thing at once.

—Samuel Smiles

Who begins too much accomplishes little.

—German proverb

Time is at once the most valuable and the most
perishable of all our possessions.

—John Randolph

There is nothing so useless as doing efficiently
that which should not be done at all.

—Peter F. Drucker

4   Making the Decision

The single most difficult aspect of a leader's job is decision making. In this section we witness the struggle, the process, and the ability to make healthy decisions that enrich our organizations and the people who work within them

A decision is process. People are successful in today's high-tech world by constantly altering and adjusting to the environment. It's a constant process of change. You can't make decisions that are absolute, because there is no absolute. There are only relative situations.

—Regis McKenna

Each time an insight or a fact is withheld and an appropriate question is suppressed, the decision making process is less than it might have been.

—Eugene Kranz

What path to take, what option to choose is easier for the leader with a firm and solid purpose and meaning in their life.

—John R. Childress

The man who never alters his opinion is like standing water, and breeds reptiles of the mind.

—William Blake

Decision Making is a process of humility, patience, and listening. At the same time you've done your homework. It's not magic.

—R. E. McMaster

Imagination is more important than knowledge.

—Albert Einstein

In almost every industry I know, the biggest breakthroughs come far afield of the conventional thinking.

—Robert Pittman

The difference between success and failure, therefore, lies not in how well you deal with the known, but how effectively you can respond to the unknown; those shadowy, more ambiguous, more uncertain components that lie out there beyond the realm of what you can see.

—Pete Dawkins

You are not here merely to make a living. You are here in order to enable the world to live more amply, with greater vision, with a finer spirit of hope and achievement. You are here to enrich the world, and you impoverish yourself if you forget the errand.

—Woodrow Wilson

The entirety of one's adult life is a series of personal choices and decisions. If we can accept this totally, then we become free people. To the extent that we do not accept this we will forever feel ourselves victims.

—M. Scott Peck

Choice, not chance, determines destiny.

—Author unknown

To doubt everything or to believe everything are two equally convenient solutions; both dispense with the necessity of reflection.

—Jules-Henri Poincaré

Committee—a group of men who individually can do nothing but as a group decide that nothing can be done.

—Fred Allen

No duty the executive had to perform was so trying as to put the right man in the right place.

—Thomas Jefferson

In a tight job market you must try to make sure that a hasty hiring decision doesn't blow up in your face.

—Michael Barrier

No one's going to be fired for making a mistake, because if you're not making mistakes, it means that you're not trying anything new.

—Robert Pittman

The key elements in the process may be neither the message nor the medium, but the source and the target.

—James MacGregor Burns

Where the willingness is great, the difficulties cannot be great.

—Nicolo Machiavelli

The greatest discovery of our generation is that a human being can alter his life by altering his attitudes.

—William James

If a man insisted always on being serious, and never allowed himself a bit of fun and relaxation, he would go mad or become unstable without knowing it.

—Herodotus

Experience is not what happens to you, but what you make of what happens to you.

—Eugene Kranz

Act boldly and unseen forces will come to your aid.

—Dorothea Brande

Do, or do not. There is no try.

—Yoda

5   Accountabiltiy and Responsibility

Being accountable for what we do, for how we relate to employees, and how we grow our organizations is an awesome responsibility. It comes with the territory of leadership and is what distinguishes a leader from a manager. What does it mean to be accountable? What are real responsibilities of leadership? Here are what some leaders think.

Leadership starts with having a very clear vision of where you are going. You must also have the ability to articulate that vision so people can understand the structure of where you are going. Leadership is not individual. It means getting things done through teamwork. Personally, I have always been much more interested in leadership than management.

—John Sculley

Managers have to switch from supervisory roles to acting as facilitators, as enablers, and as people whose jobs are the development of people and their skills so that those people will be able to perform value-adding processes themselves.

—Michael Hammer and James Champy

We will have to learn how to measure the productivity of the knowledge worker, because most people will be engaged—as they are today—not in manual production work but in varieties of tasks involving knowledge.

—Peter F. Drucker

A good manager is a man who isn't worried about his own career but rather the careers of those who work for him.

—H. S. M. Burns

For me, real leadership is how the leader behaves when no one is looking.

—John R. Childress

If it is our feelings about things that torment us rather than the things themselves, it follows that blaming others is silly. Therefore, when we suffer setbacks, disturbances or griefs, let us never place the blame on others, but on our own attitudes.

Small minded people habitually reproach others for their own misfortunes. Average people reproach themselves. Those who are dedicated to a life of wisdom, understand that the impulse to blame something or someone is foolishness, that there is nothing to be gained in blaming, whether it be others or oneself.

—Epictetus

I praise loudly, I blame softly.

—Catherine II

We are taught you must blame your father, your sisters, your brothers, the school, the teachers—you can blame anyone, but never blame yourself. It's never your fault. But it's ALWAYS your fault, because if you wanted to change, you're the one who has got to change. It's as simple as that, isn't it?

—Katherine Hepburn

Nothing serves a leader better than a knack for narrative. Stories anoint role models, impart values, and show how to execute indescribably complex tasks.

—Thomas A. Stewart

The work is often deadly and boring, but it requires a keen intelligence, and the only way I can compete with large corporations is to treat my employees better, move them up faster, give them more money and put mirrors in the bathrooms.

—James R. Uffelman

You're either part of the solution or part of the problem.

—Eldridge Cleaver

A tragic error occurs when a man who is doing a job well is promoted to a position of incompetence. It is almost impossible to unpromote him.

—Laurence J. Peter and Raymond Hull

The conventional definition of management is getting work done through people, but real management is developing people through work.

—Agha Hasan Abedi

Take care of those who work for you and you'll float to greatness on their achievements.

—H. S. M. Burns

The person who knows "how" will always have a job. The person who knows, "why" will always be his boss.

—Diane Ravitch

Competence, like truth, beauty and contact lenses, is in the eye of the beholder.

—Lawrence J. Peter

6   Principles and Values

Without values, and the principles upon which those values are based, our organizations would be rudderless. They form the basis for all action, providing the guiding vision by which we design the models that run our businesses. They speak directly to what is held closest and dearest to each of us, and they are the reason we do what we do and live our lives serving our organizations.

It is clearly necessary to invent organizational structures appropriate to the multi-cultural age. But such efforts are doomed to failure if they do not grow out of something deeper, out of generally held values.

—Vaclav Havel

Some are born great, some achieve greatness, and some have greatness thrust upon them.

—William Shakespeare

Leadership is having the courage to act.

—John R. Childress

I think it is important to have a perspective, a view of the contemporary world, from that I derive my course of action. It becomes a criteria, an overall ecological sense that we are all part of a larger system, and that we have to not only look out for our own particular well being, but we have to perceive that well being as tied up with the well being of others. So we get a sense of wholeness. That is the goal.

—Edmund "Jerry" Brown

There can be great value in being competitive— so long as you know who is on your side.

—Larry E. Senn

Try not to become a man of success but rather try to become a man of value.

—Albert Einstein

I know the price of success: dedication, hard work and an unremitting devotion to the things you want to see happen.

—Frank Lloyd Wright

The aim of education is the knowledge not of facts but of values.

—William Ralph Inge

Authentic values are those by which a life can be lived, which can form a people that produces great deeds and thoughts.

—Allan Bloom

Search men's governing principles, and consider the wise, what they shun and what they cleave to.

—Marcus Aurelius Antoninus

We have not yet met a truly successful person who wasn't actively learning about themselves every day.

—Gay Hendricks and Kate Ludeman

Every time a value is born, existence takes on a new meaning; every time one dies, some part of that meaning passes away.

—Joseph Wood Krutch

A vision not consistent with values that people live by day by day will not only fail to inspire genuine enthusiasm, it will often foster outright cynicism.

—Peter M. Senge

The shift of paradigms requires an expansion not only of our perceptions and ways of thinking, but also of our values.

—Fritjof Capra

Democracy, in one word ...is ...cooperation.

—Dwight D. Eisenhower

Between plans and reality lie years of habits, customs, unwritten ground rules, parochialism and vested interests: the corporate culture.

—Larry E. Senn and John R. Childress

Never cheat a customer, even if you can.

—A. T. Stewart

Industry without art is barbarism.

—Herbert Read

It is not the brains that matter most, but that which guides them—the character, the heart, generous qualities, progressive ideas.

—Fyodor Dostoyevski

New opinions are always suspected, and usually opposed, without any other reason but because they are not already common.

—John Locke

The pleasure you get from your life is equal to the "attitude" you put into it.

—M. Scott Peck

The deepest principle in human nature is the craving to be appreciated.

—William James

What you're thinking, what shape your mind is in, is what makes the biggest difference of all.

—Willie Mays

Employees pay more attention to values-in-use than to espoused values.

—James M. Kouzes and Barry Z. Posner

When children know that they are valued,
when they truly feel valued in the deepest parts
of themselves, then they feel valuable. This
knowledge is worth more than any gold.

—M. Scott Peck

One of the worst things we do in corporate
America is not tell people what we think
of them.

—Lawrence A. Bossidy

As a CEO, your instinct is to help employees
whose personal problems are interfering with
their job performance.

—Jeffrey L. Seglin

Most of the human beings whose lives have stirred us and whom we admire are people who dedicated themselves not to the elementary pleasures, but to something noble, something fine, something that reaches beyond. Some encounter with necessity is the ground of taking one's life seriously. It's the ground of being open to the call of something higher in which we have a chance to participate…

—Leon Kass

To be what we are, and to become what we are capable of becoming is the only end of life.

—Robert Louis Stevenson

We make a living by what we get, but we make
a life by what we give.

—Author unknown

Behind an able man there are always other
able men.

—Chinese proverb

The happiest moment of my life is now because
I am here now.

—Anthony Hopkins

If you play it safe in life, you've decided that you don't want to grow anymore.

—Shirley Hufstedler

Courage is resistance to fear, mastery of fear—not absence of fear.

—Mark Twain

Companies need to stop chasing best-in-class models for their corporate planning processes and play to their strengths instead.

—Andrew Campbell

Accountability is a state of mind—a point of view about life. It is a self-empowering view that gives us more control of our life and of our destiny.

—Larry E. Senn

Existing leaders have to live their best value system so that they are very powerful models and mentors.

—Stephen R. Covey

Tell me what company you keep, and I'll tell you what you are.

—Miguel de Cervantes

Truth is the most valuable thing we have. Let us economize it.

—Mark Twain

We must stand together; if we don't there will be no victory for any one of us.

—Mother Jones

There are two good things in life—freedom of thought and freedom of action.

—W. Somerset Maugham

If we had no faults of our own, we would not take so much pleasure in noticing those of others.

—François, Duc de La Rochefoucauld

It is impossible to truly understand another without making room for that person within yourself.

—M. Scott Peck

If you want to have a more pleasant, cooperative teenager, be a more understanding, empathetic, consistent, loving parent. If you want to have more freedom, more latitude in your job, be a more responsible, a more helpful, a more contributing employee. If you want to be trusted, be trustworthy.

—Stephen R. Covey

Live in such a way that you would not be ashamed to sell your parrot to the town gossip.

—Will Rogers

We are not our feelings. We are not our moods. We are not even our thoughts. Self-awareness enables us to stand apart and examine the way we see ourselves. It affects not only our attitudes and behaviors, but also how we see other people.

—Stephen R. Covey

Perpetual devotion to what a man calls his business, is only sustained by perpetual neglect of many other things.

—Robert Louis Stevenson

I've learned that something constructive comes from every defeat.

—Tom Landry

He who will not reason is a bigot; he who cannot is a fool; and he who dares not, is a slave.

—William Drummond

Respect is appreciation of the separateness of the other person, of the ways in which he or she is unique.

—Annie Gottlieb

The difference between greatness and mediocrity is often how an individual views a mistake.

—Nelson Boswell

Justice is never anything in itself, but in the dealings of men with one another. In any place whatever and at any time. It is a kind of compact not to harm or be harmed.

—Epicurus

If you refuse to accept anything but the best, you very often get it.

—W. Somerset Maugham

He who loses wealth loses much; he who loses a friend loses more; but he that loses courage loses all.

—Miguel de Cervantes

If you would not be forgotten as soon as you are dead, either write things worth reading or do things worth writing.

—Benjamin Franklin

"Top" management is supposed to be a tree full of owls—hooting when management heads in to the wrong part of the forest. I'm still unpersuaded they even know where the forest is.

—Robert Townsend

How wonderful it is that nobody need wait a single moment before starting to improve the world.

—Anne Frank

Never do anything against conscience even if
the state demands it.

—Albert Einstein

Talkativeness is one thing, speaking well
another.

—Sophocles

Often people attempt to live their lives back-
wards; they try to have more things, or more
money in order to do more of what they want
so they will be happier. The way it actually
works is in reverse. You must first be who you
really are, then do what you need to do, in
order to have what you want.

—Margret Young

In the business world, everyone is paid in two coins: cash and experience. Take the experience first; the cash will come later.

—Harold S. Gennen

I have no complex about wealth. I have worked hard for my money, producing things people need. I believe that the able industrial leader who creates wealth and employment is more worthy of historical notice than politicians or soldiers.

—J. Paul Getty

Money is better than poverty, if only for financial reasons.

—Woody Allen

We don't see things as they are; we see them as we are.

—Anaïs Nin

When you're an orthodox worrier, some days are worse than others.

—Erma Bombeck

7   The Shadow of the Leader

The shadow each leader casts extends throughout his or her organization. The actions and attitudes of the leader are echoed in the decisions and temperament of management and employee alike. Understanding this phenomenon is essential when guiding change and creating an environment conducive to growth and innovation.

An institution is the lengthened shadow of one man.

—Ralph Waldo Emerson

You can delegate authority, but you can never delegate responsibility for delegating a task to someone else. If you picked the right man, fine, but if you picked the wrong man, the responsibility is yours—not his.

—Richard E. Krafve

The measure of a man is not the number of his servants but in the number of people whom he serves.

—Paul D. Moody

It is easy to have calmness in inactivity, it is hard to have calmness in activity, but calmness in activity is true calmness.

—Shunryu Suzuki

The secret of winning football games is working more as a team, less as individuals. I play not my eleven best, but my best eleven.

—Knute Rockne

He who has never learned to obey cannot be a good commander.

—Aristotle

A great man is willing to be little.

—Ralph Waldo Emerson

No man has any right to rule who is not better than the people over whom he rules.

—Cyrus

I must follow the people; am I not their leader?

—Benjamin Disraeli

The buck stops here.

—Harry Truman

A frightened captain makes a frightened crew.

—Lister Sinclair

The executive exists to make sensible exceptions to general rules.

—Elting E. Morison

The true leader is always led.

—C. G. Jung

If the coach is organized, everything falls into place. If he has self-discipline, the team has discipline. If he's dedicated, the team is dedicated. Everything revolves around the head coach. He's the one who has to make the team go.

—Ray Nitschke

He that would govern others first should be the master of himself.

—Philip Massinger

Next to doing a good job yourself, the greatest joy is in having someone else do a first-class job under your direction.

—William Feather

Fail to honor people, they fail to honor you. But of a good leader, who talks little, when his work is done, his aim fulfilled, they will all say, "We did this ourselves."

—Lao-Tzu

Executives who get there and stay suggest
solutions when they present problems.

—Malcolm S. Forbes

If you have knowledge, let others light their
candles by it.

—Margaret Fuller

A leader has the vision and conviction that a
dream can be achieved. He inspires the power
and energy to get it done.

—Ralph Lauren

Leadership: The art of getting someone else to do something you want done because he wants to do it.

—Dwight D. Eisenhower

Authority ...is in itself inherently an act of imagination.

—Richard Sennett

Take rest; a field that has rested gives a beautiful crop.

—Ovid

There is nothing which we receive with so much reluctance as advice.

—Joseph Addison

It is much easier to be critical than correct.

—Benjamin Disraeli

Managers are people who never put off till tomorrow that which they can get someone else to do today.

—Author unknown

There is such a rebound from parental influence that it generally seems that the child makes use of the directions given by the parent only to avoid the prescribed path.

—Margaret Fuller

Why are we doing what we do? What are the expectations we have for our organizations and the realities that temper them? How do we find satisfaction without paying the toll charged by stress and pressure? Here are some leaders who have attempted to answer these questions and perhaps posed some new ones for us to ponder.

All organizations have cultures. The only choice we have is whether we shape them or they shape us.

—Larry E. Senn

The real leader has no need to lead—he is content to point the way.

—Henry Miller

A company has a better chance of making a difference if it knows how its business agenda relates to social needs.

—Rosabeth Moss Kanter

The greatest mistake you can make is to be continually fearing that you'll make one.

—Elbert Hubbard

There are two kinds of success. One is the very rare kind that comes to the man who has the power to do what no one else has the power to do. That is genius. But the average man who wins what we call success is not a genius. He is a man who has merely the ordinary qualities that he shares with his fellows, but who has developed those ordinary qualities to a more than ordinary degree.

—Theodore Roosevelt

Always leave enough time in your life to do something that makes you happy, satisfied, or even joyous. That has more of an effect on economic well being than any other single factor.

—Paul Hawken

Effective leaders are alike in one crucial way: they all have a huge degree of emotional intelligence.

—Daniel Goleman

A manager manages, but only a human soul gifted with imagination has the resilient artistry to live and work with forces that call for deeper strategies than containment.

—David Whyte

For a leader, taking the confident and courageous step to "yes" is a confirming demon-
stration of one's grounding in purpose
and meaning.

—John R. Childress

Creativity is so delicate a flower that praise
tends to make it bloom, while discouragement
often nips it in the bud. Any of us will put out
more and better ideas if our efforts are
accepted.

—Alexander F. Osborn

One of the most important results you can
bring into the world is the you that you really
want to be.

—Robert Fritz

It is the province of knowledge to speak and it is the privilege of wisdom to listen.

—Oliver Wendell Holmes

He that will have his son have respect for him and his orders, must himself have a great reverence for his son.

—John Locke

The Chinese word for crisis consists of two characters: one represents "danger" and the other "hidden opportunity."

—M. Scott Peck

The typical successful American businessman
was born in the country, where he worked
like hell so he could live in the city, where he
worked like hell so he could live in the country.

—Don Marquis

The reason why worry kills more people than
work is that more people worry than work.

—Robert Frost

Take care to get what you like or you will be
forced to like what you get.

—George Bernard Shaw

The most important thing about goals is having one.

—Geoffrey F. Abert

The first problem for all of us, men and women, is not to learn but to unlearn.

—Gloria Steinem

All of the significant battles are waged within the self.

—Sheldon Kopp

One can never consent to creep when one feels an impulse to soar.

—Helen Keller

When you cease to make a contribution you begin to die.

—Eleanor Roosevelt

Management is more art than science. No one can say with certainty which decisions will bring the most profit, any more than they can create instructions over how to sculpt a masterpiece. You just have to feel it as it goes.

—Richard D'aveni

All progress is based upon a universal innate desire on the part of every organism to live beyond its income.

—Samuel Butler

No man needs sympathy because he has to work.... Far and away the best price that life offers is the chance to work hard at work worth doing.

—Theodore Roosevelt

There is only one success—to be able to spend your life in your own way.

—Christopher Morley

You don't get to choose how you're going to die. Or when. You can only decide how you're going to live. Now.

—Joan Baez

It has been a thousand times observed,
and I must observe it once more, that the
hours we pass with happy prospects in view,
are more pleasing than those crowned
with fruition.

—Oliver Goldsmith

I never did anything worth doing by accident;
nor did any of my inventions come by accident;
they came by work.

—Thomas Alva Edison

To be organized and efficient, to live wisely, we
must daily delay gratification and keep an eye
on the future; yet to live joyously we must also
possess the capacity, when it is not destructive,
to live in the present and act spontaneously.

—M. Scott Peck

I find the great thing in this world is not so much where we stand, as in what direction we are moving. To reach the port of heaven, we must sail sometimes with the wind and sometimes against it—but we must sail, and not drift, nor lie at anchor.

—Oliver Wendell Holmes

There are two ways of spreading light: to be the candle or the mirror that reflects it.

—Edith Wharton

I do not think that I will ever reach a stage when I will say, "This is what I believe. Finished." What I believe is alive ...and open to growth....

—Madeline L'Engle

Better keep yourself clean and bright; you are the window through which you must see the world.

—George Bernard Shaw

Problems are only opportunities in work clothes.

—Henry J. Kaiser

Always treat your employees exactly as you want them to treat your best customers.

—Stephen R. Covey

The first and greatest commandment is, Don't let them scare you.

—Elmer Davis

Goals must be deadlined to be taken seriously
and to provide a sense of urgency.

—Alec Mackenzie

The future is not in the hands of Fate,
but in ours.

—Author unknown

In order to gain and to hold the esteem of men it
is not sufficient merely to possess wealth or
power. The wealth or power must be put in evidence, for esteem is awarded only on evidence.

—Thorstein Veblen

Desire creates the power.

—Raymond Holliwell

There is always room at the top.

—Daniel Webster

Money itself isn't the primary factor in what one does. A person does things for the sake of accomplishing something. Money generally follows.

—Henry Crown

There are two things to aim at in life: first, to get what you want; and, after that, to enjoy it. Only the wisest of mankind achieve the second.

—Logan Pearsall Smith

To have a reason to get up in the morning, it is necessary to possess a guiding principle.

—Judith Guest

As adults, our choices are almost unlimited, but that does not mean they are not painful. Frequently our choices lie between the lesser of two evils, but it is still within our power to make these choices.

—Author unknown

While others may argue about whether the
world ends with a bang or a whimper, I just
want to make sure mine doesn't end with
a whine.

—Barbara Gordon

My favorite thing is to go where I've
never been.

—Diane Arbus

Throw out the words, "If I can," "I hope,"
"Maybe," and replace them with "I can," "I
will," "I must."

—Author unknown

Don't fear failure so much that you refuse to try new things. The saddest summary of a life contains three descriptions: could have, might have, and should have.

—Louis E. Boone

There are risks and costs to a program of action, but they are far less than the long-range risks and costs of comfortable inaction.

—John F. Kennedy

Do not persist, then, to retain at heart one sole idea, that the thing is right which your mouth utters, and nought else beside.

—Sophocles

I had rather be hissed for a good verse than applauded for a bad one.

—Victor Hugo

Failure is the opportunity to begin again more intelligently.

—Henry Ford

Often the difference between a successful man and a failure is not one's better abilities or ideas, but the courage that one has to bet on his ideas, to take a calculated risk —and to act.

—Maxwell Maltz

You may be disappointed if you fail, but you are doomed if you don't try.

—Beverly Sills

...it's just ...ironic. A stutterer becomes an actor. Sometimes when we exercise our weakest muscle it becomes our strongest muscle.

—James Earl Jones

You've got to be very careful if you don't know where you are going, because you might not get there.

—Yogi Berra

9   The Current of Change

That change is a constant has almost become cliché, but then ideas normally become cliché because they are true. In an era when industries often measure time in dog-years, our organizational systems must be open to change and adaptation in order to survive. But change does not always equate to upheaval and revolution. As we are learning, real change is evolutionary. Nonetheless, it still requires courage to take the next evolutionary step, no matter how necessary it is to survive.

To stay mentally alert and engaged during
a 50-year working life, one must know how
and when to change the work one does.

—Peter F. Drucker

Nothing endures but change.

—Heraclitus

What most fundamentally characterizes the
well-adjusted, or highly sane person is not
chiefly the particular habits or attitudes that
he holds, but rather the deftness with which
he modifies them in response to changing
circumstances.

—Wendell Johnson

Either we obsolete ourselves, or the competition will.

—Economist

The sure path to oblivion is to stay where you are.

—Bernard Fauber

Change is the law of life and those who look only to the past or present are certain to miss the future.

—John F. Kennedy

The world hates change, yet it is the only thing that has brought progress.

—Charles F. Kettering

Progress is impossible without change; and those who cannot change their minds cannot change anything.

—George Bernard Shaw

When all think alike, then no one is thinking.

—Walter Lippmann

A man's mind, stretched by a new idea, can never go back to its original dimensions.

—Oliver Wendell Holmes Jr.

Change means the unknown…. It means too many people cry insecurity. Nonsense! No one from the beginning of time has had security.

—Eleanor Roosevelt

Things do not change; we change.

—Henry David Thoreau

To truly change the corporation, you need to change the culture

—Larry E. Senn and John R. Childress

In today's business world, where change is occurring so furiously, effective leaders keep a very focused eye on the competition and quickly make necessary adjustments to their team to be successful.

—Maureen O'Brien

For the times they are a changin'.

—Bob Dylan

Life belongs to the living, and he who lives must be prepared for changes.

—Johann Wolfgang von Goethe

If we want to change a situation, we first
have to change ourselves. And to change
ourselves effectively, we first have to change
our perceptions.

—Stephen R. Covey

Changing the direction of a large company
is like trying to turn a aircraft carrier. It takes
a mile before anything happens. And if it was
a wrong turn, getting back on course takes
even longer.

—Al Ries

Everyone thinks of changing the world, no one
thinks of changing himself.

—Leo Tolstoy

People handle their fear of change in different ways, but the fear is inescapable if we are in fact to change.

—M. Scott Peck

I have accepted fear as a part of life—specifically the fear of change…. I have gone ahead despite the pounding in the heart that says: turn back…

—Erica Jong

Science can amuse and fascinate us all—but it is engineering that changes the world.

—Isaac Asimov

All things must change ...to something new,
to something strange.

—Henry Wadsworth Longfellow

As the world endlessly changes, so must we. The
greatest power we have is the ability to envision
our own fate—and to change ourselves.

—Noel M. Tichy and Stratford Sherman

The most distinguished hallmark of American
society is and always has been change.

—Eric Sevareid

In today's economy even getting laid off could turn out to be the best thing that ever happened to you.

—Maureen Quinn

One never goes so far as when one doesn't know where one is going.

—Johann Wolfgang von Goethe

10   Interactions, Teamwork, and Strategies

If we are unable to create healthy interactions within our organizations, we will never have the teamwork required to fulfill our strategies. When we look at the great teams of champions in sports, there is certainly individual talent, but most of all there is a willingness to work together toward a common purpose and follow an aligned strategy. We see it in every aspect of life, from the smallest interactions of the particles of the atom to the largest human organizations, the whole is always greater than the sum of its parts.

I not only use all the brains I have, but all
I can borrow.

—Woodrow Wilson

We must dare to think "unthinkable" thoughts.
We must learn to explore all the options and
possibilities that confront us in a complex and
rapidly changing world. We must learn to wel-
come and not fear the voices of dissent. We
must dare to think about "unthinkable" things
because when things become unthinkable,
thinking stops and action becomes mindless.

—William Fulbright

A team is a small number of people with complementary skills who are committed to a common purpose, performance goals, and an approach for which they hold themselves mutually accountable.

—Jon R. Katzenback and Douglas Smith

As simple as they may seem, praise and thanks still are the most neglected social gestures in the workplace.

—Brenda Paik Sunoo

Those who bring sunshine to the lives of others, cannot keep it from themselves.

—James Barrie

The surest way for an executive to kill himself is to refuse to learn how and when, and to whom to delegate work.

—James Cash Penney

Companies don't have strategies. They have ongoing strategic conversations by a body of people. Out of these ongoing conversations, decisions are made.

—Stewart Brand

If I had to choose one quality to distinguish the best new leaders, it is openness to criticism, the passion for continual self-development, which teaches the leader to value the development of others.

—Michael Maccoby

Empowerment is meaningless unless people have access to information. The goal of our technology strategy is to make sure that the information is available on the desktop of the person who is doing the job.

—Bill Eaton

The greater the contrast, the greater the potential. Great energy only comes from a correspondingly great tension between opposites.

—C. G. Jung

Two heads are better than one.

—John Heywood

98 percent of the battle is listening and paying attention. When a worker has a good idea, you do something.

—Walter E. Goddard

Under the team system, there's no place to hide and eventually everything becomes apparent.

—Michael Hammer

The secret of a winning culture is building high performance teams.

—Larry E. Senn and John R. Childress

Hear the other side.

—Saint Augustine

If you want to be listened to, you should put in time listening.

—Marge Piercy

When you get an idea, listen to it.

—Robert Pittman

If we want to be heard we must speak in a language the listener can understand and on a level at which the listener is capable of operating.

—M. Scott Peck

The most important measure of how good a game I'd played was how much better I'd made my teammates play.

—Bill Russell

I don't get a big charge out of being the leading scorer…. I just do what has to be done for us to win. That might be anything at anytime— defense, rebounding, passing. I get satisfaction out of being a team player.

—Kareem Abdul-Jabbar

I believe we (the 49ers) were able to accomplish what we did because the players believed in each other. Each man was an extension of each other, like a chain link fence. Our players learned to make sacrifices, to put it on the line for the guys 15 yards away (on the sideline).

—Bill Walsh

My best friend is the one who brings out the best in me.

—Henry Ford

Individual commitment to a group effort—that is what makes a team work, a company work, a society work, a civilization work.

—Vince Lombardi

Just because you're a leader, doesn't mean your team knows when, how, why, and where to follow.

—Julie Bick

We are a partnership or nothing.

—Woodrow Wilson

It were not best that we should all think alike; it is difference of opinion that makes horse races.

—Mark Twain

Often we can help each other most by leaving each other alone. At times we need the hand-grasp and the word of cheer.

—Elbert Hubbard

There must be a division not only of profits, but a division also of responsibilities.... We must insist upon labor sharing the responsibilities for the result of the business.

—Louis D. Brandeis

In case of dissension, never dare to judge till you've heard the other side.

—Euripides

When there's too much tension or too little communication between sales and marketing, business is bound to suffer.

—Sara Lorge

Our knowledge is the amassed thought and experience of innumerable minds.

—Ralph Waldo Emerson

No culture can live if it attempts to be exclusive.

—Mahatma Gandhi

No snowflake in an avalanche ever feels responsible.

—Stanislaw Jerzy Lec

We must all hang together or assuredly we shall all hang separately.

—Benjamin Franklin

He that walketh with wise men shall be wise.

—Bible, Proverbs 13:20

Many hands make light work.

—John Heywood

Good company in a journey makes the way seem shorter.

—Italian proverb

Men fundamentally can no more get along
without direction than they can without eating,
drinking, or sleeping.

—Charles de Gaulle

Let us never negotiate out of fear; but let us
never fear to negotiate.

—John F. Kennedy

It seems to me that trying to live without
friends is like milking a bear to get cream for
your morning coffee. It is a whole lot of trouble, and then not worth much after you get it.

—Zora Neale Hurston

It's always worthwhile to make others aware of their work.

—Malcolm S. Forbes

Listen to your customers and take their bad news as an opportunity to turn your failures into the concrete improvements they want.

—Bill Gates

There is no such whetstone, to sharpen a good wit and encourage a will to learning, as is praise.

—Roger Ascham

For all the money we spend on marketing,
we know very little about our customers.

—Robert Thomas

The key to community is the acceptance
—in fact the celebration—of our individual
and cultural differences. It is also the key
to world peace.

—M. Scott Peck

E-mail and voice mail are efficient, but face-
to-face contact is still essential to true communication.

—Edward M. Hallowell

Living In A
Complex World

We are discovering that the level of interactions within our organizations has become incredibly complex. We have individuals communicating with individuals, work teams communicating with other teams, departments with other departments, and divisions with other divisions. Yet in many cases, all it takes to stall the process is one person digging his or her feet in the sand and getting stuck in their own personal point of view. We all want a simpler world, but whether we like it or not, the world is complex. Learning to adapt and remain unstuck within the complexity is what we learn from the leaders that follow.

Nothing is simple anymore. Nothing is stable.
The business environment is changing before
our eyes, rapidly, radically, perplexingly.

—James Champy

Our thinking creates problems which the same
level of thinking can't solve.

—Albert Einstein

The reasonable man adapts himself to the
world, the unreasonable one persists to adapt
the world to himself. Therefore all progress
depends on the unreasonable man.

—George Bernard Shaw

Past success does not account for current
conditions.

—Howard Sherman and Ron Schultz

We live between two dense clouds—the forget-
ting of what was and the uncertainty of what
will be.

—Anatole France

Every man takes the limits of his own field
of vision for the limits of the world.

—Arthur Schopenhauer

Equilibrium is death

—John H. Holland

A great many people think they are thinking
when they are merely rearranging their
prejudices.

—William James

If the only tool you have is a hammer, you
tend to see every problem as a nail.

—Abraham Maslow

If anything goes bad, I did it.
If anything goes semi-good, then we did it.
If anything goes real good, then you did it.
That's all it takes to get people to win football
games.

—Paul "Bear" Bryant

All change is a miracle to contemplate; but it is
a miracle which is taking place every instant.

—Henry David Thoreau

He who never made a mistake, never made
a discovery.

—Samuel Smiles

Our culture has historically focused on independence and on the individual being right. In these complex times, the focus should be on winning through collaborative efforts.

—Larry E. Senn

Discovery is seeing what everybody else has seen and thinking what nobody else has thought.

—Albert Szent-Gyorgyi

First we shape our institutions, and afterwards they shape us.

—Winston Churchill

People like to think that businesses are built of numbers (as in the "bottom-line"), or forces (as in "market forces"), or things ("the product"), or even flesh and blood ("our people"). But that is wrong.... Businesses are made of ideas—ideas expressed as words.

—James Champy

Experience never errs, what alone may err is our judgement, which predicts effects that cannot be produced by our experiments.

—Leonardo da Vinci

Power does not corrupt men; fools, however, if they get into a position of power, corrupt power.

—George Bernard Shaw

The art of life lies in a constant readjustment to our surroundings.

—Kakuzo Okakura

One of the difficult problems that women decision makers run into when they trust their intuition is that the men they work with don't.

—Roberta Williams

The best bosses have to be smart. Like the center on a football team, they've got to know what's going on behind their backs.

—Sal F. Marino

It's hard to fight an enemy who has outposts in your head.

—Sally Kempton

Things are seldom what they seem. Skim milk masquerades as cream.

—William S. Gilbert

Two men look out through the same bars: One sees the mud, and one the stars.

—Frederick Langbridge

It may be those who do most, dream most.

—Stephen Leacock

The ability to subordinate an impulse to a value is the essence of the proactive person. Reactive people are driven by feelings, by circumstances, by conditions, by their environment. Proactive people are driven by values—carefully thought about, selected, and internalized values.

—Stephen R. Covey

Life is the art of drawing sufficient conclusions from insufficient premises.

—Samuel Butler

To understand everything is to forgive everything.

—Madame de Staël

Saying is one thing and doing is another.

—Montaign

Never before have we had so little time in which to do so much.

—Franklin D. Roosevelt

We're on the edge of a revolution out here. All over the country, people are fed up with getting on planes and finding out that the person next to them paid one-tenth of what they paid.

—Kevin Stamper

We judge ourselves by what we feel capable of doing, while others judge us by what we have already done.

—Henry Wadsworth Longfellow

Call it a clan, call it a network, call it a tribe, call it a family. Whatever you call it, whoever you are, you need one.

—Jane Howard

We need to better respect and value differences. Too many people go through life thinking everyone else has the same style they do but the others are "defective."

—Larry E. Senn

Nothing will ever be attempted if all possible objections must be first overcome.

—Samuel Johnson

When a group of monks asked a rabbi for advice on saving their dying order, he responded, "I am sorry. The only thing I can tell you is that the Messiah is one of you." Pondering this, the old monks began to treat each other, and themselves, with extraordinary respect on the off chance that one of them might be the Messiah.

—M. Scott Peck

12   Reflections and Beliefs

Our beliefs lead directly to the results we produce. When we allow ourselves the space to reflect on the world we encounter—as the leaders in this section have—and then open to the new possibilities that emerge, our results improve. The key is the time for reflection, during which we can recognize where we might be locked into our own personal beliefs that could keep us from discovering a new way of viewing our work and our working together.

Whatever is felicitously expressed risks being worse expressed: it is a wretched taste to be gratified with mediocrity when the excellent lies before us.

—Isaac Disraeli

A corporate culture that constantly repeats the word *excellence* to itself must still have end-less reservoirs of mediocrity on which to draw, and is deathly afraid of facing up to this fact.

—David Whyte

More men are killed by overwork than the importance of the world justifies.

—Rudyard Kipling

The road up and the road down are one and the same.

—Heraclitus

People don't do business with you because you're a geek and can do regressions in your head. They come to do business with you because they like you.

—James Lee

All experience is an arch, to build upon.

—Henry Adams

A good listener is not only popular everywhere, but after a while he knows something.

—Wilson Mizner

Well-timed silence hath more eloquence
than speech.

—Martin Farquhar Tupper

He who laughs, lasts.

—Robert Fulghum

Behavior is a mirror in which every one
displays his own image.

—Johann Wolfgang von Goethe

Each day, and the living of it, has to be a con-
scious creation in which discipline and order are
relieved with some play and pure foolishness.

—May Sarton

The most important discoveries, the greatest
art, and the best management decisions come
from taking a fresh look at what people take
for granted or cannot see precisely because
it is too obvious.

—Richard Farson

I do not try to dance better than anyone else.
I only try to dance better than myself.

—Mikhail Baryshnikov

They who dream by day are cognizant of
many things which escape those who dream
only by night.

—Edgar Allen Poe

Nothing contributes so much to tranquilize the mind as a steady purpose—a point on which the soul may fix its intellectual eye.

—Mary Wollstonecraft Shelley

There are two kinds of light—the glow that illuminates and the glare that obscures.

—James Thurber

Personally I'm always ready to learn, though I do not always like being taught.

—Winston Churchill

As I grow older, I pay less attention to what men say, I just watch what they do.

—Andrew Carnegie

Human improvement is from within outward.

—James Froude

People in more and more organizations are asking their leaders to better "walk their talk."

—Larry E. Senn

Nothing in life is to be feared. It is only to be understood.

—Marie Curie

I don't think much of a man who is not wiser today than he was yesterday.

—Abraham Lincoln

We are what we repeatedly do. Excellence then is not an act, but a habit.

—Aristotle

Learning is discovering that something is possible.

—Fritz Perls

The happiness of your life is in direct proportion to the character of your thoughts.

—Author unknown

Corporate risk takers are very much like entrepreneurs. They take personal risks to make new ideas happen.

—Gifford Pinchot III

Innovation is the specific instrument of entre-
preneurship ...the act that endows resources
with a new capacity to create wealth.

—Peter F. Drucker

A bad attitude is the worst thing that can
happen to a group of people. It's infectious.

—Roger Allan Raby

In a hierarchy every employee tends to rise
to his level of incompetence.

—Laurence J. Peter and Raymond Hull

A little uncertainty is good for everything.

—Henry Kissinger

People spend what's in a budget, whether they need it or not.

—George W. Sztykiel

The apple does not fall far from the tree.

—American proverb

He who goes with wolves learns to howl.

—Spanish proverb

You can live a lifetime and at the end of it, know more about other people than you know about yourself.

—Beryl Markham

I must govern the clock, not be governed by it.

—Golda Meir

Success is a journey, not a destination.

—Ben Sweetland

The only limit to growth in the services business are skills and people.

—Sam Albert

The employer puts his money into business and the workman his life. The one has as much right as the other to regulate that business.

—Clarence S. Darrow

The difference between failure and success is doing a thing nearly right and doing a thing exactly right.

—Edwards Simmons

Even the frankest and bravest of subordinates do not talk with their boss the same way they talk with colleagues.

—Robert Greenleaf

When the environment goes down the tubes,
the market itself won't be far behind.

—Ray Anderson

There is no greater bane to friendship than
adulation, fawning, and flattery.

—Marcus Tullius Cicero

You can always spot a well-informed man—his
views are the same as yours.

—Ilka Chase

My idea of an agreeable person is a person
who agrees with me.

—Benjamin Disraeli

Flattery is praise without foundation.

—Eliza Leslie

I have received memos so swollen with managerial babble that they struck me as the literary equivalent of assault with a deadly weapon.

—Peter Baida

Every man's work, whether it be literature, music, or pictures of architecture or anything else, is always a portrait of himself.

—Samuel Butler

13   The Enterprising Spirit

What drives us forward? What possesses us to move toward success? These leaders attempt to capture the essence of what success requires of us and what it demands we let go of in order to sustain it.

Vision is the art of seeing something invisible.

—Jonathan Swift

No man ever yet became great by imitation.

—Samuel Johnson

A man is known by the company he organizes.

—Ambrise Bierce

In order to survive, we must break tradition.

—Walter E. Goddard

Some of the most exciting jobs of the future are the ones that haven't been created yet.

—Faith Popcorn and Lys Marigold

He who is not courageous enough to take risks will accomplish nothing in life.

—Mohammad Ali

Progress always involves risk; you can't steal second base and keep your foot on first.

—Frederick Wilcox

Make every decision as if you owned the whole company.

—Robert Townsend

We are not victims of the world we see. We are victims of the way we see the world.

—Author unknown

Wisdom is the power to put our time and our knowledge to the proper use.

—Thomas J. Watson

All the troubles of man come from his not knowing how to sit still.

—Blaise Pascal

The strongest of all warriors are these two; time and patience.

—Leo Tolstoy

You grow up the day you have your first real laugh at yourself.

—Ethel Barrymore

The greater part of our happiness or misery depends on our dispositions and not on our circumstances.

—Martha Washington

Pay no attention to what critics say. A statue has never been erected in honor of a critic.

—Jean Sibelius

Never lose a chance of saying a kind word.

—William Makepeace Thackeray

Write down the advice of him who loves you, though you like it not at present.

—English proverb

Procrastination is the art of keeping up with yesterday.

—Don Marguis

You can't escape the responsibility of tomorrow by evading it today.

—Abraham Lincoln

We may affirm absolutely that nothing great in the world has ever been accomplished without passion.

—Georg Hegel

Do not look where you fell, but where you slipped.

—African proverb

Failure is success if we learn from it.

—Malcolm S. Forbes

What would you attempt to do if you knew you could not fail?

—Robert Schuller

Every man is the architect of his own fortune.

—Appius Claudius Caecus

The best way to predict the future is to create it.

—Peter F. Drucker

The golden opportunity you are seeking is in yourself. It is not in your environment; it is not in luck or chance, or the help of others; it is in yourself alone.

—Orison Swett Marden

A healthy high-performance culture is the greatest asset an organization or team can have.

—Larry E. Senn and John R. Childress

Author Index

A

Abedi, Agha Hasan, 63

Abert, Geoffrey F., 106

Adams, Henry, 161

Addison, Joseph, 96

Afer, Publius Terentius, 42

African proverb, 179

Albert, Sam, 169

Ali, Mohammad, 175

Allen, Fred, 52

Allen, Woody, 31, 86

American proverb, 168

Anderson, Ray, 171

Antoninus, Marcus Aurelius, 69

Arbus, Diane, 115

Aristotle, 91, 166

Ascham, Roger, 143

Asimov, Isaac, 126

Augustine, Saint, 135

B   Bacon, Francis, 31, 36

Baez, Joan, 108

Baida, Peter, 172

Banks, Sydney, 6

Barrie, James, 131

Barrier, Michael, 53

Barrymore, Ethel, 177

Baryshnikov, Mikhail, 163

Behn, Sally, 32

Berra, Yogi, 118

Beveridge, W. I., 22

Beverly Sills, 118

Bible, Proverbs, 13:20, 141

Bick, Julie, 138

Bierce, Ambrise, 174

Blake, William, 49

Blinder, Alan, 43

Bloom, Allan, 69

Bombeck, Erma, 87

Boone, Louis E., 32, 116

Bossidy, Lawrence A., 74

Boswell, Nelson, 82

Bovee, Courtland, 44

Brand, Stewart, 132

Brande, Dorothea, 55

Brandeis, Louis D., 139

Brown, Edmund "Jerry," 67

Browne, Thomas, 16

Bruyère, Jean de la, 31

Bryant, Paul "Bear," 149

Burns, H. S. M., 59, 63

Burns, James MacGregor, 53

Butler, Samuel, 107, 154, 172

C

Caecus, Appius Claudius, 180

Campbell, Andrew, 77

Campbell, Joseph and Moyers, Bill, 12

Camus, Albert, 24, 35

Capra, Fritjof, 70

Carlson, Richard, 3, 5, 7, 9, 10, 14, 19

Carlson, Richard and Bailey, Joseph, 3, 7, 9

Carnegie, Andrew, 164

Carter, Jimmy, 31

Catherine II, 60

Champy, James, 58, 146, 151

Charles, Elizabeth Rundle, 8

Chase, Ilka, 171

Childress, John R., 23, 38, 49, 59,
66, 71, 103, 123, 134, 180

Chinese proverb, 30, 76

Churchill, Winston, 150, 164

Cicero, Marcus Tullius, 171

Cleaver, Eldridge, 62

Colvin, Geoffrey, 29

Conner, Daryl R., 27

Covey, Stephen R., 35, 36, 78, 80,
81, 111, 125, 154

Crown, Henry, 113

Curie, Marie, 165

Cyrus, 92

D   D'aveni, Richard, 107

da Vinci, Leonardo, 151

Darrow, Clarence S., 170

Davis, Elmer, 111

Dawkins, Pete, 50

de Cervantes, Miguel, 78, 83

de Gaulle, Charles, 142

de Staël, Madame, 154

DiMaggio, Joe, 28

Disney, Walt, 26

Disraeli, Benjamin, 92

Disraeli, Isaac, 160

Dostoyevski, Fyodor, 72

Drucker, Peter F., 23, 46, 59, 120, 167, 180

Drummond, William, 82

Dyer, Wayne, 26

Dylan, Bob, 124

E Eaton, Bill, 133

Economist, 121

Edison, Thomas Alva, 109

Einstein, Albert, 50, 146

Eisenhower, Dwight D., 71, 96

Eliza Leslie, 172

Emerson, Ralph Waldo, 15, 90, 92, 140

English proverb, 178

Epictetus, 7, 16, 60

Ertol, Danny, 42

Euripides, 139

F Farson, Richard, 163

Fauber, Bernard, 121

Feather, William, 94

Finkelstein, Louis, 39

Fletcher, Jerry, 30

Forbes, Malcolm S., 95, 143, 179

Ford, Henry, 117, 137

Ford, Henry, 117, 137

France, Anatole, 147

Frank, Anne, 84

Franklin, Benjamin, 32, 42, 43, 84,
141

Fritz, Robert, 103

Frost, Robert, 105

Froude, James, 165

Fulbright, William, 130

Fulghum, Robert, 162

Fuller, Buckminster, 4

Fuller, Margaret, 95, 97

G   Gandhi, Mahatma, 140

Gates, Bill, 143

Gauguin, Paul, 28

Gennen, Harold S., 86

German proverb, 46

Getty, J. Paul, 86

Gilbert, William S., 153

Goddard, Walter E., 134, 174

Goldsmith, Oliver, 16, 109

Goleman, Daniel, 4, 15, 18, 102

Author Index

Gordon, Barbara, 115

Gottlieb, Annie, 82

Greenleaf, Robert, 170

Guest, Judith, 114

H
Hallowell, Edward M., 144

Hamilton, Alexander, 44

Hammer, Michael, 58, 134

Hammer, Michael and Champy,
    James, 58

Hanh, Thich Nhat, 11

Havel, Vaclav, 66

Hawken, Paul, 102

Hegel, Georg, 179

Heider, John, 2

Hendricks, Gay and Ludeman,
    Kate, 69

Hepburn, Katherine, 61

Heraclitus, 120, 161

Herodotus, 54

Heywood, John, 133, 141

Holland, John H., 148

Holliwell, Raymond, 113

Holmes, Oliver Wendell, 104, 110,
    122

Holmes, Oliver Wendell, Jr., 122

Holtz, Lou, 28

Hopkins, Anthony, 76

Horace, 28, 29

Howard, Jane, 156

Hubbard, Elbert, 101, 139

Hufstedler, Shirley, 77

Hugo, Victor, 27, 117

Hurston, Zora Neale, 142

I   Iacocca, Lee, 39

Inge, William Ralph, 68

Italian proverb, 141

J   Jackson, Phil, 13, 17

James, William, 54, 73, 148

Jefferson, Thomas, 52

Johnson, Samuel, 157, 174

Johnson, Wendell, 120

Jones, James Earl, 118

Jones, Mother, 79

Jong, Erica, 126

Jung, C. G., 93, 133

K   Kaiser, Henry J., 41, 111

Kanter, Rosabeth Moss, 100

Kass, Leon, 75

Katzenback, Jon R. and Smith,
Douglas, 131

Keller, Helen, 106

Kempton, Sally, 153

Kennedy, John F., 22, 116, 121, 142

Kettering, Charles F., 121

Kipling, Rudyard, 160

Kissinger, Henry, 25, 168

Knight, Philip, 41

Kolbe, Kathy, 40

Kopp, Sheldon, 106

Kouzes, James M. and Posner, Barry Z., 73

Krafve, Richard E., 90

Kranz, Eugene, 48, 55

Krishnamurti, J., 2, 5, 10, 13, 20

Krutch, Joseph Wood, 70

L L'Engle, Madeline, 110

Landiak, Mark, 33

Landry, Tom, 81

Langbridge, Frederick, 153

Lauren, Ralph, 95

Leacock, Stephen, 153

Lec, Stanislaw Jerzy, 140

Lee, James, 161

Lessing, Doris, 43

Lincoln, Abraham, 165, 178

Lippmann, Walter, 25, 122

Locke, John, 72, 104

Lombardi, Vince, 137

Longfellow, Henry Wadsworth,
16, 127, 156

Lorge, Sara, 140

M   Maccoby, Michael, 132

Machiavelli, Nicolo, 54

Mackenzie, Alec, 112

Mallarmé, Stéphane, 25

Maltz, Maxwell, 117

Marden, Orison Swett, 180

Marguis, Don, 178

Marino, Sal F., 152

Markham, Beryl, 169

Maslow, Abraham, 148

Massinger, Philip, 94

Maugham, W. Somerset, 79, 83

Mays, Willie, 73

McKenna, Regis, 48

McMaster, R. E., 49

Meir, Golda, 169

Midler, Bette, 33

Miller, Dan, 18

Miller, Henry, 100

Mizner, Wilson, 161

Montaign, 155

Moody, Paul D., 90

Morison, Elting E., 93

Morley, Christopher, 108

Murry, John Middleton, 22

N   Nietzsche, Friedrich Wilhelm, 24

Nin, Anaïs, 87

Nitschke, Ray, 93

Norwegian proverb, 35

O   O'Brien, Maureen, 124

Okakura, Kakuzo, 152

Osborn, Alexander F., 103

Ovid, 96

P   Pascal, Blaise, 176

Peck, M. Scott, 29, 51, 72, 74, 80, 104, 109, 126, 135, 144, 157

Penney, James Cash, 40, 132

Perls, Fritz, 166

Peter, Lawrence J., 64

Peter, Laurence J. and Hull, Raymond, 62, 167

Phillips, Michael, 45

Piercy, Marge, 135

Pinchot, Gifford III, 166

Pirsig, Robert M., 17

Pittman, Robert, 50, 53, 135

Plotinus, 11

Poe, Edgar Allen, 163

Popcorn, Faith and Marigold, Lys, 175

Q   Quinn, Maureen, 128

R   Raby, Roger Allan, 167

Randolph, John, 46

Ravitch, Diane, 63

Read, Herbert, 71

Ries, Al, 125

Rockne, Knute, 91

Rogers, Will, 80

Roosevelt, Eleanor, 107, 123

Roosevelt, Franklin D., 155

Roosevelt, Theodore, 101, 108

Russell, Bill, 136

S   Saint Teresa of Avila, 5

Samples, Bob, 9

Sanders, Jerry, 39

Sarton, May, 162

Schiller, J. C. F. von, 15

Schopenhauer, Arthur, 147

Author Index

Schuller, Robert, 179

Sculley, John, 58

Seglin, Jeffrey L., 74

Senge, Peter M., 3, 8, 70

Senn, Larry E., v, vii, x, 38, 67, 71,
    78, 100, 123, 134, 150, 156, 165,
    180

Senn, Larry E. and Childress, John
    R., 38, 71, 123, 134, 180

Sennett, Richard, 96

Sevareid, Eric, 127

Shakespeare, William, 9, 36, 66

Shaw, George Bernard, 30, 105,
    111, 122, 146, 151

Shelley, Mary Wollstonecraft, 164

Sherman, Howard and Schultz,
    Ron, 27, 147

Sibelius, Jean, 177

Simmons, Edwards, 170

Sinclair, Lister, 92

Smiles, Samuel, 46, 149

Smith, Elinor, 34

Smith, Logan Pearsall, 114

Sophocles, 85, 116

Spanish proverb, 168

Stamper, Kevin, 155

Steinem, Gloria, 106

Stern, Lawrence, 12

Stevenson, Robert Louis, 75, 81

Stewart, A.T., 71

Stewart, Thomas A., 61

Strehlo, Kevin, 40

Sunoo, Brenda Paik, 131

Suzuki, Shunryu, 38, 91

Sweetland, Ben, 169

Swift, Jonathan, 174

Syrus, Publilius, 22, 29, 45

Sztykiel, George W., 168

T   Thackeray, William Makepeace,
   178

Thomas, Robert, 144

Thoreau, Henry David, 26, 123,
   149

Thurber, James, 164

Tichy, Noel M., and Sherman,
   Stratford, 127

Tolstoy, Leo, 125, 176

Townsend, Robert, 84, 175

Toynbee, Arnold, 14

Tracy, Brian, 24

Author Index

Truman, Harry, 92

Trungpa, Chögyam, 6, 13, 19

Tupper, Martin Farquhar, 162

Twain, Mark, 77, 79, 138

U   Uffelman, James R., 62

Underhill, Evelyn, 33

V   Valery, Paul, 11

Veblen, Thorstein, 112

von Goethe, Johann Wolfgang,
     124, 128, 162

W   Walsh, Bill, 137

Walton, Izaak, 41

Ward, William Arthur, 34

Washington, Martha, 177

Watson, Thomas J., 176

Webster, Daniel, 113

Wharton, Edith, 110

Whyte, David, 102, 160

Wilber, Ken, 10

Wilcox, Frederick, 175

Williams, Roberta, 152

Wilson, Woodrow, 51, 130, 138

Wright, Frank Lloyd, 68

Y   Yoda, 55

Young, Margret, 85

About Senn-Delaney Leadership

The Senn-Delaney Leadership Consulting Group was founded in 1978 with a specific mission: Assist CEOs and senior executives to create High-performance Teams and Winning Cultures. Today, Senn-Delaney Leadership is a global firm known for its experience and accomplishments in the areas of Culture-Shaping, Teambuilding and Leadership Development. While management consultants work on formulating strategy, structure, systems, and processes, we as leadership consultants focus on creating the organizational and team effectiveness needed to ensure those change initiatives work.

High-performance teams and winning cultures are of utmost importance today. Research and experience confirm that the shortfall in most change initiatives is due to the human issues, not the technical ones. This is true for mergers, new leaders, new strategies, restructures, IT installations and all other major changes.

For over 20 years, we've worked with corporate leaders in the Energy, Information Technology, Financial Services, and Consumer Products/Diversified industries. Our clients include: Bell Atlantic, Pacific Bell, Sprint, British Telecom, British Gas, Commonwealth Edison, Portland General Electric, Florida Power and Light, Compaq Computer, IBM PC Division, Hewlett Packard, McDonald's U.S., PepsiCo, Bank One, GTE Information Services and Rockwell International. We have also aided the merger and acquisition transition process within organizational recombinations such as: Chemical-Chase Bank, OhioEdison-Centerion, Southwestern Bell-Pacific Bell Directory, Compaq-Digital and BankOne-Chicago First and National Bank of Detroit.

As we approach and enter the new millennium, the professionals of the Senn-Delaney Leadership Consulting Group remain committed to our vision of "Making a Difference Through Leadership."

For additional information about the consulting services of Senn-Delaney Leadership, please contact us at our corporate headquarters:

Senn-Delaney Leadership Consulting Group, Inc.
3780 Kilroy Airport Way, Long Beach, CA 90806
Phone (562) 426-5400 Fax (562) 436-5174
E-mail: book_info@sdlcg.com